The **Mayflower** is certainly the oldest tug in Britain. She was built by Stothert & Marten at Hotwells in Bristol in 1861 for use on the canal that links Gloucester and Sharpness. Her original owner was a Timothy Hadley, towage contractor for the Gloucester and Berkeley Canal Company which became the Sharpness New Docks & Gloucester & Birmingham Navigation Co in 1874 and took over Hadley's vessels. In 1899 her original single-cylinder vertical steam engine was replaced by a vertical compound condensing engine and this is geared to a single screw. To allow passage beneath bridges further up the non-tidal River Severn, her funnel was hinged in 1906 and a wooden wheelhouse was fitted in the late 1930s. Ownership passed to British Waterways in 1948. She remained in use until 1964 and was then laid up and sold two years later. She sank in Gloucester Docks in 1977 but escaped demolition and in 1981 was bought by the City of Bristol Museum and Art Gallery. She has been completely renovated as a working exhibit. We see her in the City Docks on 16 February 2014.

(Chris Jones)

1

Ideally this tug should have appeared in *Volume 1* as she was originally in the C J King fleet but in reality she was not quite ready for inclusion in that book although she was present at the launch of *Volume 1* at the South West Ship Show on 18 April 2015. She has the distinction of being the first diesel tug in the fleet of C J King. Built as **Volunteer** in 1934 by Charles Hill & Son of Bristol, she has a British Polar K56 diesel engine. Sold in 1959 to F A Ashmead & Son Limited, she was renamed **Robert A** and continued to work in Bristol's City Docks and on the River Avon. She was photographed in the Bristol Channel in June 1982.

(Bernard McCall collection)

The **Robert A** was later laid up in Gloucester and sold in 1983 to Drake Towage in Wisbech, by whom she was renamed **Sea Fitter**. She was sold to another owner in Wisbech in 1999 and reverted to **Robert A**. In 2002, she was sold to a Mr Patterson, moved to Whitehaven and she took her original name of **Volunteer**. She was then bought by her present owner, Dave Elms, who is restoring her to near-original condition and has brought her back to Bristol. She was photographed as she passed through the lock and into the Cumberland Basin on her return to her home port in March 2015 with her owner on the deck of his tug.

(Bernard McCall)

The **Ernest Brown** was an example of a "TID" tug built during World War 2. She was launched at the Richard Dunston shipyard in Thorne on 5 June 1944 and delivered as **TID 95** during August. After service for the Ministry of War Transport, she was bought in 1946 by T R Brown & Sons, of Bristol, and was re-engined in 1964, her compound steam engine of 220ihp steam engine being replaced by a 6-cylinder Ruston & Hornsby engine of 225bhp. She was later acquired by Evans Marine Ltd, of Maidenhead, and in 1986 was reported to have been sent to work on a civil engineering project on the River Seine near Paris. She was then sold to a French group for restoration in 1993 and in 1996 she attended a sailing ship regatta in Brest but she never left and was abandoned in a ships' graveyard at Landévennec. On 15 April 2010 she was lifted out of the water and transported to the Guyot Environment Company to be broken up.

(Danny Lynch)

Powered by a Polar diesel engine of 310bhp, the *Finch* was built as *Falconbrook* in 1956 at the Richard Dunston shipyard in Thorne. Owned by River Lighterage Co Ltd, of Brentford, she passed to another Thames-based owner in 1966. This was Alf White who renamed her *Boys White* in the following year. Around 1969 she was renamed *Finch* and passed to the ownership of the Fleetwood Fishing Vessel Owners' Association and worked as the dock tug at Fleetwood. In 1978 she moved from one fishing port to another when bought by Talisman Trawlers Ltd, of Lowestoft. Laid up in Lake Lothing in August 1983, she was bought a year later by Mike Mayhew, of Bristol. She is seen in the City Docks on 30 April 1986. In the following year she was bought by Captain D McKenzie in Ullapool in order to assist the larger trawlers that were then berthing and landing at the Scottish port.

(The late Mike Hawkins, Chris Jones collection)

This small tug was based in Bristol only briefly. She was built as *Gertrud* at the Voorwaarts shipyard in West-Graftdijk for Dutch owners based in Dordrecht. Her engine was a 6-cylinder "De Industrie" of 300bhp. She came into British ownership in 1962 when acquired by Tilbury Contracting & Dredging Co Ltd. Renamed *Pullwell* she passed through the hands of Westminster Dredging, Poole-based Frank Pearce Tugs and Ham

Dredging before being bought by Mike Mayhew in Bristol in 1983. Later in that same year she was bought by owners in Torquay and was renamed *Mainpull*. She was photographed at Hotwells on 11 October 1983. Bought by a Southampton owner in 2005 she was renamed *Susie B* and was reported to have been laid up at Southampton in 2005.

(Cedric Catt)

The diminutive **Mainscrew** was built in 1982 at the David Abels shipyard in Bristol where she was yard number 11. The yard fabricated the steel work only as the tug was fitted out by her owners, Mayhew Marine. She was powered by a Foden FD4 engine of 110bhp and was credited with a bollard pull of 2.2 tonnes. In the late 1990s, the tug was sold to a company based on the River Clyde and was renamed **Owl Tug**. This company went into liquidation about 2010 and all assets were sold at auction. The tug is understood to have been broken up in 2012.

(The late Mike Hawkins, Chris Jones collection)

7

The **Cabot** was built in 1952 and replaced the steam tug **Bulldog**. Owned by the Port of Bristol Authority, she was used for moving grain elevators and barges rather than ship towing. Here we see her at Avonmouth towing the dredger **Evenlode** on 1 September 1971. She was built locally at the Charles Hill shipyard and was fitted with two 3-cylinder British Polar diesel engines. These were replaced by two 8-cylinder Gardner engines in 1963. She was equipped with a fine saloon for use by the mayoral team on their annual inspections. In 1974 she was sold to Maritime & Salvage Ltd, of Kingston-upon-Thames, and then to Lowestoft-based Winney Towing Ltd. In August 1983 she returned to Maritime Towing & Salvage Ltd and operated by McCann Tugs Ltd. About this time, she was used to assist the construction work for a new breakwater at Douglas, Isle of Man, and she was also used as a spectator boat at the annual Oxford/Cambridge boat race. She was sold to an Irish owner in 1986 and broken up in Ireland in 1995.

(John Wiltshire)

The **Resolute Lady** was built by G K Stothert in Bristol in 1897 and was originally named **Resolute**. She is understood to have been ordered by the Sharpness Dockyard Company. Ownership subsequently passed to British Waterways via the British Transport Commission and then in 1970 to F A Ashmead & Sons, tug and barge owners based in Bristol by whom she was renamed **Thelm Leigh**. In 1957 her original Stothert steam engine was replaced with a 6-cylinder Ruston & Hornsby engine of 380bhp and with a nominal bollard pull of 4 tonnes. On Christmas Day 1977 she sank in the Old Dock at Avonmouth after being hit by a coaster. She was raised on 16 January of the following year and was bought by Fred Larkham who restored her to working condition with the name **Resolute Lady**. We see her at Avonmouth on 5 October 1988.

(Peter Hobday)

During World War 2, a total of 182 tugs of a type known as TIDs were built. The *TID 15* was launched at the Richard Dunston shipyard at Thorne on 10 June 1943. Between delivery two months later and the end of the war, she worked for both the US navy and the Ministry of War Transport. In 1949 she was sold to Benjamin Perry & Sons Ltd, Bristol, and renamed *BP II*, becoming *Salisbury* in 1958. Six years later, her original 2-cylinder compound steam engine of 220ihp was replaced by a 6-cylinder turbocharged Ruston & Hornsby engine of 365bhp which was geared to a 4-bladed bronze propeller. She had a bollard pull of just over 5 tonnes. The work was carried out at the Charles Hill shipyard in Bristol. In 1980, following the cessation of the Bristol Steam Navigation Company's service between Avonmouth and Dublin, she was sold to dealers but remained laid up in the Old Dock at Avonmouth. Sold to the Laxey Towing Company in 1981, she was the best tug ever owned by the company but had to be replaced because she was too underpowered to handle the larger ferries entering service for the Isle of Man Steam Packet Co Ltd. She was sold to Hunter Marine, of Wicklow, in 1992 and she was eventually broken up at Castletownbere in the Republic of Ireland in 2010.

(John Wiltshire)

In the late 1960s, a new generation of tanker appeared, namely Very Large Crude Carriers (VLCCs), which would serve only a limited number of ports. The Gulf Oil Corporation constructed a huge storage and transfer facility at Whiddy Island, Bantry Bay, in the south-west of Ireland. R & J H Rea won the contract to provide tugs for this new terminal and four firefighting tugs were built for the Bantry Bay Towing Co Ltd. Two were built at the Richard Dunston yard in Hessle and two by C D Holmes in Beverley. The first of the Dunston pair was the **Dingle Bay**. She was launched on 17 January 1968 and completed on 1 May. Power came from a 6-cylinder Mirrlees engine of 2521bhp geared to a fixed pitch propeller in a steerable Kort nozzle and providing a bollard pull of 37 tonnes. On 8 January 1979, an explosion on the tanker **Betelgeuse** berthed at Whiddy Island caused huge damage and Gulf closed the terminal. The four tugs were sent to lay up at Milford Haven but later served other ports, notably the Clyde. In 1998 the **Dingle Bay** was sold to owners in Cameroon for service at Douala. She was renamed **Centaure** but there is no recent news about her. We see her alongside the Charles Hill shipyard for repairs to serious engine and crankshaft damage.

(Danny Lynch)

The **New Ross 1** was completed by Arklow Marine in 1986 and was used mainly to handle barges filled with silt dredged from the bed of the River Barrow at New Ross. She also assisted vessels without bow thrusters which called at that Irish port. On 8 August 1995 she capsized while assisting a tanker arriving at Great Island Power Station. Both of her crewmen sadly died in the incident. She was salved and rebuilt with a Caterpillar engine of 550bhp geared to a single screw in a Kort nozzle. This gave her a bollard pull of 7 tonnes. After purchase by Cardiff Commercial Boat Operators, she was used to support civil engineering projects and occasionally to escort vessels navigating the River Avon to or from Bristol. On 17 March 2009, new lock gates were delivered on a barge and we see the **New Ross 1** entering the lock at the end of the voyage with the barge in tow.

(Bernard McCall)

An example of the Pushycat 1500 standard design, the **Bristolian** was built at the Gorinchem yard of Damen Marine Services and completed as **Zal 4** in early December 1979. Her 12-cylinder Caterpillar engine of 550bhp gives her a bollard pull of just over 5 tonnes. In July 1980 she was acquired by Dordrecht-based Rederij T Muller and was renamed **En Avant 9**. In mid-2003 she came into British ownership when bought by H & S Marine for whom she worked as **Herman Jr**. Bought by Bristol City Council in 2007 and renamed **Bristolian**, she is an ideal vessel for escorting larger vessels using the River Avon in addition to more general duties within the City Docks which, although seeing virtually no commercial shipping, still require constant maintenance. She was photographed in the River Avon during the delivery of the new lock gates seen in the previous photograph.

(Bernard McCall)

13

A product of the Damen shipyard at Hardinxveld, this tug was completed in 1988 as **Frances** for the Holyhead Towing Company but was soon renamed **Afon Wen**. Power comes from two 8-cylinder Caterpillar engines geared to twin fixed pitch propellers in steerable Kort nozzles. This combination gives her a bollard pull of 13 tonnes. She entered the Cory fleet in March 1999 and was renamed **Forager** after the company won a contract to provide marine services at the Butinge oil terminal in Lithuania. On completion of the contract she was sent to the Bristol Channel in June 2005 to be used mainly as an escort vessel in the River Avon. She was photographed in the river and heading towards Bristol on 21 July 2005. She saw very little use and by 2007 she had moved to the Lindø shipyard near Odense in Denmark.

(Dominic McCall)

The return to Bristol of Brunel's mighty ship **Great Britain** on 7 July 1970 was a notable occasion. Two tugs assisting the **Great Britain** were featured separately in *Volume 1* but we felt that the occasion deserved special mention in this volume.

On the bow of the **Great Britain** was C J King's **Sea Alert,** dating from 1960 whilst the same company's **John King** was amidships and ready to give assistance into the lock. This was the final commercial duty of the **John King**, now happily preserved and restored in the City Docks.

(Bernard McCall collection)

On the stern was the **Falgarth** of R & J H Rea dating from 1958. We are unsure about the continued existence of this tug. She was noted laid up at the Greek port of Eleusis as **Kapetan Napoleon** in August 2013.

(Bernard McCall collection)

This interesting tug was launched at the Appledore yard of P K Harris (Shipbuilders) Ltd on 18 July 1958 and delivered as **Hazelgarth** to Rea Towing Ltd at Liverpool on 11 May 1959. She was innovative in several ways. Tankers using the River Mersey were increasing rapidly in numbers and size. The Rea company insisted that the builder should design the superstructure of the tug in order to ensure adequate visibility when handling the larger tankers. A second innovation was her name. A decision had been taken that Rea's Mersey tugs would henceforth have the name of a tree prefixing "garth". She was sold out of the Rea fleet in 1988 and was renamed **Mister Cornishman** the following year by West Coast Towage Ltd. We see her as such towing a barge in the River Avon. A further sale saw her become **Shaula** in 1990 and then **Tommy Dev** in 1994. Later in 1994 she was sold to operators in the Somali Republic and departed for Mogadishu after being refurbished at Husband's shipyard in Southampton. There is no certain further information.

(Danny Lynch)

The **MCS Lenie** was built in 1997 at the David Abels shipyard in Bristol for Maritime Craft Services. She was on her delivery voyage when photographed in the River Avon in August 1997. In April 2008 she was sold to Serco Denholm Ltd and was renamed **SD Kyle of Lochalsh**. She had already been on contract to the Ministry of Defence. She is based at the the British Underwater Test and Evaluation Centre (BUTEC) range at Kyle which is used to evaluate the sensors and aural emissions of British submarines. The **SD Kyle of Lochalsh** is used mainly to support submarine trials off the Isle of Skye. She is driven by two Caterpillar main engines with a total output of 2230bhp and geared to two fixed pitch propellers giving her a bollard pull of 26 tonnes.

(Danny Lynch)

The David Abels shipbuilding yard was opened in 1980 on part of the site of the former Charles Hill Albion yard that closed in 1977. The first two vessels built were tugs for Larne-based John McLoughlin (Shipping) Ltd. In 2004, the company returned to Abels for the construction of two new vessels to be used mainly for towage and line handling. Awaiting delivery to their owner, the **Noleen McLoughlin** and barely visible **Leanne McLoughlin** were photographed in July 2005. They are fitted with Volvo engines and they have a 4 tonne bollard pull. The McLoughlin company was founded in 1970 by John McLoughlin senior and remains in family control with his son John and daughters Donna, Deirdre and Adrienne now involved.

(Bernard McCall)

We now move to the docks at the mouth of the Avon. Seen undergoing bollard pull trials in Royal Portbury Dock on 25 September 1992, the **Harald** was built by Appledore Shipbuilders. She was launched on 28 August 1992 and was delivered in the following month to Orkney Towage Limited. This company was established in 1976 mainly to provide towage services at the Flotta oil terminal, then operated by Occidental, and receiving some of the first flows of crude oil from North Sea fields. This was the third of the company's three tugs, the two previous tugs having been built at the McTay yard at Bromborough. Power comes from two 6-cylinder Ruston engines each of 2202bhp and geared to two Aquamaster stern-mounted propulsion units. This combination gives her a bollard pull of 55 tonnes.

(Danny Lynch)

The silt-laden waters of the Bristol Channel mean that the port approaches require constant dredging. Plough dredging at the entrance to Avonmouth on 14 March 2013 was the *Janette B*. Her hull was built at the Damen subsidiary shipyard at Kozle in Poland and the vessel was completed at the Damen yard in Hardinxveld with delivery in April 2008. Power comes from two 12-cylinder Caterpillar engines, each of 885bhp and geared to two fixed-pitch propellers in Van der Giessen optima nozzles. This gives her a bollard pull of 22 tonnes. She was sold in July 2013 and was renamed *Marineco India*.

(Chris Jones)

The hull of the Andre B was constructed at the Hoebee shipyard in Dordrecht with completion in April 2008 at the Zwijndrecht yard of Gebroeders Kooiman. Power comes from two 16-cylinder Mitsubishi engines, each of 1700bhp and geared to two fixed pitch propellers in Hodi nozzles. This combination gives her a bollard pull of 45 tonnes. She arrived at Royal Portbury Dock on 30 September 2012 towing Skyline Barge 17 on to which would be loaded the inner lock gates which were removed for overhaul.

(Chris Jones)

21

The **Ada-D** is an example of a particular type of tug known as an anchor handling tug. At the stern, such vessels have rollers over which anchors may be discharged or raised. The rollers can be seen clearly in this photograph taken when handling a barge in Royal Portbury Dock on 3 June 2008. Power comes from two 12-cylinder MWM engines, each of 571bhp and geared to two fixed pitch propellers. This gives her a bollard pull of 27 tonnes. She was built by IMC at Tonnay-Charente in France and initially traded as **Amarante** under the flag of Panama. In 1990, she hoisted the German flag and was renamed **Salus**, becoming **Ada-D** after purchase by Smit Transport Europe in 1997. In 2011 she was sold within the Netherlands and was renamed **Marian-V**. Her appearance was altered by the removal of her funnel casing with only two small uptakes now visible.

(Kevin Jones)

Of very distinctive appearance, the **Yogi** is an example of a multipurpose vessel known as a multicat and specifically is of the Multicat 2611 design. Delivered by the Damen shipyard in Hardinxveld in May 2008, she can be used for anchor handling, dredging, windfarm support, diving support and, of course, towing. She is driven by three 12-cylinder Caterpillar engines with a total output of 2435bhp and geared to three fixed pitch propellers in van der Giessen Optima nozzles. This combination gives her a bollard pull of 30 tonnes. She is owned by Herman Senior, based in the Dutch port of Dordrecht. The **Yogi** had **Skyline Barge 20** in tow when photographed on 20 May 2013.

(Chris Jones)

The **MTS Indus** has a rather unusual history. Her original name was **Drydock** and this gives a clue to her early history. She was built by the Wilton-Fijenoord shipyard (Dok- en Werf- Maatschappij Wilton-Fijenoord) at Schiedam. Launched on 28 July 1964, she commenced work at her builder's shipyard some three months later and remained there for two decades. In mid-July 1984, she was acquired by Smit International and was renamed **Smit Azie**. She became **Azie Tug** in November 1988 following sale to Damen Marine Services but this name lasted only 14 months as a sale within the Netherlands saw her become **Indus** in December 1989. In 2008 she was acquired by the rapidly-expanding MTS Group, based in Falmouth, and was renamed **MTS Indus**. When built, she had a 6-cylinder MAN engine of 890bhp which gave her a bollard pull of 11 tonnes. In 2002, however, she was extensively refitted. A bow thruster was added and a new engine was installed, this being a 12-cylinder Caterpillar of 1776bhp. This is geared to a fixed pitch propeller in a Kort nozzle and gives her a bollard pull of 24 tonnes. She was towing a jack-up barge when photographed on 25 November 2010.

(Chris Jones)

In recent years, various designs of multipurpose tugs have appeared, suitable not only for towage but also to support civil engineering projects of many kinds. One of these designs is termed Shoalbuster. It was the Damen yard at Hardinxveld that completed a hull built in Poland and delivered it to a subsidiary company as **DMS Heron** on 2 November 2006. An example of Damen's Shoalbuster 2308 design, the vessel was handed over on 26 November 2006 to the MTS Group and renamed **MTS Valour**. Her two 12-cylinder Caterpillar engines with a total power of 1746bhp are geared to two fixed pitch propellers and give a 21 tonne bollard pull. She is seen arriving at Avonmouth on 13 March 2013 with the barge **Terra Marique** in tow.

(Chris Jones)

The **MTS Victory** was acquired by the MTS Group from Norwegian tug operator Bugser og Berging in March 2011. She was built at the 'De Lastdrager' shipyard of W Visser & Zoon in Den Helder and was originally named **Haabas**. She became **Multi Mammut** in 2000. Power comes from a single 12-cylinder Alco engine of 2719bhp geared to a controllable pitch propeller in a steerable nozzle. She has a bollard pull of 35 tonnes. We see her at Avonmouth on 13 March 2013.

(Chris Jones)

The **MTS Viscount** was launched at the Cochrane shipyard in Selby on 7 April 1977 and delivered to Humber Tugs as **Lady Moira** on 8 November. After twenty years service on the Humber she was bought by Terneuzen-based Multraship and was renamed **Multratug 7**. She entered the MTS fleet as **MTS Viscount** in February 2011. She is driven by two 8-cylinder Ruston engines, each of 1460bhp and geared to two fixed pitch propellers in Kort nozzles. This gives her a bollard pull of 52 tonnes. The MTS Group has expanded its fleet and its activities immensely over the last decade and this tug was noted working in the Brazilian port of Santana during autumn 2014. We see her towing **Skyline Barge 20** in Royal Portbury Dock on 19 September 2012.

(Chris Jones)

The **Carew Castle** was the second of four tugs ordered by R & J H Rea in 1958 to assist oil tankers at the new installations being built in Milford Haven. Originally named **Thorngarth**, she was launched at the Hessle yard of Henry Scarr Ltd on 28 January 1958 and completed on 17 December. In 1983 she was sold to Pounds Marine Shipping Ltd, of Portsmouth, and was laid up with engine damage. In late 1990 she was sold to Haven Maritime Ltd, Pembroke Dock, and, now repaired, was renamed **Carew Castle** and was operated by West Coast Towing. Subsequent sales saw her become **Karew Castle** (1994), **Carew Castle** once again (1996) and finally **Falmouth Bay** (1997). She was broken up at La Coruña in Spain in August 2011. The A-frame at the stern suggests that she had been undertaking plough dredging when photographed on 24 September 1992. In the background are the caravan sites of Redcliffe Bay.

(Danny Lynch)

This may well have been the only occasion that a tug from the Adsteam fleet visited our local area. The **Sun London** was launched at the Richard Dunston shipyard at Hessle on 19 July 1977 and was completed for the Alexandra Towing Company on 11 November. Her 12-cylinder Ruston engine of 2640bhp was geared to a controllable pitch propeller and this gave her a bollard pull of 45 tonnes. Alexandra was taken over by Howard Smith in 1996 and this company was in turn taken over by Adsteam in 2001. She left British ownership when sold to Sweden in 2006 but there was no change of name until 2009 when a further sale saw her become **Serval** for a Polish operator. She remains in service on general contract work throughout northern Europe. She was photographed passing Battery Point in March 2003.

(Dominic McCall)

The **Smit Orca** was built at the Barkmeijer shipyard at Stroobos in the north of the Netherlands. Launched on 9 September 1983 and delivered as **Orca** on 2 December, she became **Smit Orca** in April 1986. She is driven by two 7-cylinder MAN engines totalling 1750bhp and geared to two controllable pitch propellers. This gives her a bollard pull of 30 tonnes. She is classed as a diving support vessel. We see her passing Battery Point at Portishead on 13 November 1997 and towing the floating sheerleg **Taklift 1** which was to undertake work on the new Severn road bridge.

(Bernard McCall collection)

By the early 20th century, Egbert Wagenborg was a hugely successful entrepreneur whose businesses were based on shipping and timber transport in the Netherlands. The name Wagenborg now dominates road transport, shipping and warehousing in the northern part of the Netherlands and has been honoured with the title Royal Wagenborg. In addition to owning cargo ships and ferries, the company operates a small fleet of tugs which undertake coastal towage in addition to harbour towage at the port of Delfzijl. The tugs' names are prefixed by "Water" and the *Watergeus* called at Royal Portbury Dock on 12 May 2008. The hull of the tug was built by Stocznia Tczew in Poland and the vessel was completed at the Damen shipyard in Gorinchem. She is driven by two 12-cylinder Wärtsilä engines each of 887bhp and geared to two fixed pitch propellers. This combination gives her a bollard pull of 25.5 tonnes.

(Kevin Jones)

Like so many tugs completed at the Damen shipyard in Hardinxveld, the hull of this vessel was subcontracted and was in fact built at a shipyard in Gdynia. The **Bever** is an example of the Shoalbuster 3612 design, the biggest vessel to be built at the Hardinxveld yard. She is powered by two 16-cylinder Caterpillar engines with a total power of 5222bhp and geared to two fixed pitch propellers. This combination gives her a bollard pull of 70 tonnes. She was built for Dutch owners and in mid-March 2015 was sold to Iskes & Zoon, a company best known for harbour towage in the IJmuiden area but which has expanded into offshore work in recent years. She is seen passing Battery Point on 24 June 2014 at the start of a voyage to Mostyn.

(Bernard McCall)

The first volume of *Bristol Tugs in Colour* included a photograph of an Italian tug called **Uran** which should not be confused with the Polish tug of the same name seen here. The hull of this **Uran** was built at the SevMash shipyard at Severodvinsk in northern Russia with construction completed at the Damen yard in Gorinchem. She was handed over to Polish owner Port-Hol, based in Szczecin, in September 2001 and since 2008 she has been operated within the fleet of Fairplay Towage following that company's purchase of Port-Hol. She is driven by two 16-cylinder Caterpillar engines, each of 2291bhp and driving two directional propellers. She has a bollard pull of 54 tonnes. We see her on 30 May 2005 as she passed Battery Point on the approach to Royal Portbury Dock. She was towing the barge **Bolle VIII** on which was a new coal unloader.

(Danny Lynch)

31

The Belgian tug **Fighter** was photographed on 13 September 2006 as she towed the semi-submersible barge **Smit Anambas** carrying a crane to be used at the bulk terminal in Royal Portbury Dock. The tug was launched by Scheepswerf van Rupelmonde on 8 March 1977 and delivered in April to Antwerp-based Unie van Redding en Sleepdienst (URS). She was designed for both harbour towage and offshore work.

(Bernard McCall)

One of the most memorable duties for the **Fighter** was her role in the tragic loss of the ferry **Herald of Free Enterprise** at Zeebrugge on 6 March 1987. Her crew assisted in the rescue of many survivors and the tug was also used to deliver bodies to the shore. She was taken out of service in 2007 and, after being stripped, was towed to Rotterdam where she was to be used as a base for students of performing arts but also with an exhibition detailing her history. Little work appears to have been done to achieve these aims and she currently languishes in Rotterdam in poor external condition.

(Bernard McCall)

There could hardly have been a more suitable tug to bring the Kone coal unloader than this Finnish tug named *Kraft*. The hull of the tug was built by Herfjord Slip & Verksted with completion by Bolsones Verft at Molde in Norway. The owner was Kone crane manufacturing company. Named *Kone* and delivered in May 1976, she towed barges carrying the company's products to their intended locations. In 1979, Kone decided to outsource its transport and the *Kone* was sold to Finnish tug owner Alfons Håkans whose company was growing rapidly.

(Kevin Jones)

Renamed *Kraft*, this was the most powerful tug in the fleet for many years and Håkans agreed that it would be used to tow barges for Kone. This was, of course, in addition to other work. The *Kraft* has a 16-cylinder Nohab engine of 3520bhp which drives a fixed pitch propeller. In the late 1990s, she was chartered by Dutch operator Kotug (Adriaan Kooren).

(Kevin Jones)

A fairly regular arrival at Avonmouth and Sharpness in recent years has been the **Terra Marique**, a barge specially built to carry heavy lifts. Her local calls are usually to carry items of equipment to and from power stations. Although self-propelled in confined areas, the barge has to be towed on seagoing voyages. On 8 November 2007 it was the Dutch-owned tug **North** that was used. This tug was completed at the Kian Juan shipyard in Miri, Malaysia, during April 2007 and was launched as

Donga North 9. Power comes from two 8-cylinder Caterpillar engines each of 1024bhp geared to two fixed pitch propellers in nozzles. For the latter part of the delivery voyage from Malaysia she diverted to the Black Sea and collected the hull of the cargo ship **Victoriadiep** for delivery from Kerch in Ukraine to the Netherlands.

(Kevin Jones)

The **Pantodynamos** was launched at the Schichau shipyard in Bremerhaven on 27 November 1970 and completed as Seetrans I in April 1971 for F C H Stark, of Hamburg. Sold to other Hamburg owners in 1975, she was renamed **Raga I** and became **Hanseatic** following purchase by Petersen & Alpers in 1979. Eight years later she joined the Fairplay fleet as **Fairplay XIV** and was sold to Greek owners in 2007 when she became **Pantodynamos**. She is driven by two Atlas MaK 8-cylinder engines, each of 2393bhp and geared to a fixed pitch propeller. This gives her a bollard pull of 60 tonnes. We see her arriving at Avonmouth on 13 August 2013. The reason for her visit is explained on page 37.

(Chris Jones)

The **Warrior III** is a much-travelled tug. She was built by Kanagawa Zosen at Kobe for Japanese owners and was delivered as **Hayakuni Maru** on 10 June 1975. Power comes from two 6-cylinder Niigata engines totalling 2600bhp and driving twin stern-mounted Z-peller units. This combination gives her a bollard pull of 37 tonnes. In 1990 she was sold to owners in Setubal and hoisted the Portuguese flag as **Montenovo**. Three years later, she was acquired by Celtic Tugs Ltd and renamed **Celtic Warrior**. In mid-February 1996 she was bought by Cory Towage, renamed **Warrior**, and was immediately used in the salvage of the tanker **Sea Empress** which had grounded at Milford Haven. Once this work had been completed she was returned to Cork for rebuilding. After completion she transferred to the UK flag as **Warrior III**, the name **Warrior** being already registered. She was based on the Clyde but came to the Bristol Channel in late December 2005 to cover for a temporary shortage of local tugs, her first job being to assist with the docking of the bulk carrier **SD Nova** on 26 December. We see her at speed off Portishead on 5 January 2006.

(Dominic McCall)

The final work for the **Warrior III** in the Bristol Channel took place on 8 January and she then returned to the Clyde. Her efficient central heating certainly endeared her to her local Bristol master during her stay. She moved to Milford Haven in 2010 but saw little work and by 2013 she was laid up in Avonmouth. She was renamed **Christos XXV** on 13 August 2013 and she left Avonmouth the next day heading for Piraeus towed by **Pantodynamos** as we noted on page 35. She is clearly not in the best external condition and the Svitzer logo on her funnel has been replaced by a letter S, her new owner being Michail Spanopoulos.

(Chris Jones)

Military tugs are rarely seen in the upper part of the Bristol Channel. A most unusual vessel to pass Battery Point at Portishead on 25 May 2005 was the US Army tug **M G Anthony Wayne**, the initials M G standing for Major General. She was on passage to Sharpness where she was to be drydocked for gritblasting and painting. She is the third of a class of six large tugs built in 1994. The hulls of the tugs were built at the yard of Robert E Derecktor, Middletown, Rhode Island, with completion by Trinity/Halter Marine, Moss Point, MS. When in service, the tugs experienced stability problems. Because of this they could work only under certain conditions and always needed fuel as ballast. A modification programme was undertaken by the US Army's Combat Equipment Battalion at Hythe on Southampton Water. This tug was the prototype for modifications on the other examples.

(Bernard McCall)

The salvage tug **Cyclone** was launched at the Leith yard of Henry Robb on 10 September 1942 and she was delivered to the Admiralty as HMS **Growler** in March 1943. In 1947 she was chartered to operators in Hong Kong and renamed **Caroline Moller**, becoming **Castle Peak** for a further charter in 1952. Two years later she was returned to the Ministry of Defence and renamed **Growler**. Between 1958 and 1963 she was chartered by United Towing, Hull, and renamed **Welshman**, becoming **Cyclone** when returned to the Admiralty on 23 October 1963. Laid up at Gibraltar in 1977 she was sold to a company based in Georgetown, Cayman Islands, in April 1983 and was renamed **Martial** for work at Mombasa. She was broken up at Gadani Beach, Pakistan, in 1985. Sadly the date of the photograph is unknown as is the reason for her presence at Canon's Marsh.

(Bernard McCall collection)

Completed at the Rosetti Marino shipyard in Ravenna during May 2003, the **Braveheart** is very much a multipurpose tug as she is designed for salvage, anchor handling, firefighting, escort, tanker handling and deepsea towage. Power comes from two 9-cylinder Wärtsilä engines, each of 2133bhp geared to two Rolls-Royce fully azimuthing Aquamaster propulsion units. This gives her a bollard pull of 103 tonnes. After delivery to Portuguese operators based on the island of Madeira, her first role was in assisting tankers using a Tatl-Fina-Elf offshore mooring point. We see her approaching Avonmouth on 5 January 2009 after she had towed the **Bebedouro** back to port. The fruit juice tanker had departed for Rotterdam the previous day but broke down off Lundy Island and the **Braveheart** was summoned from Swansea to tow her back.

(Chris Jones)

In the mid-1990s, a fleet of tugs was rapidly built up in South Wales under the management of West Coast Towing (UK) Ltd. Having won the contract to handle bulk carriers visiting Port Talbot, West Coast Towing (UK) Ltd soon challenged local operators Alexandra in Swansea and Cory in Newport. They found it more difficult to obtain work on this side of the Channel. For conventional shiphandling the company bought several relatively new tugs built in Russia. We see the *Albert K* along with *Capt I B Harvey* as they assist *Evangelos G* at Avonmouth on 11 July 1999. The *Albert K* is an example of the Project 04983 design from the Gorokhovets shipyard. Originally named *Imakon 2*, she became *Albert K* for West Coast Towing (UK) Ltd. Like several other fleet mates, she returned to Russian ownership in 2003 and she was renamed *Atoll*. A tug of this name sank in the Sea of Azov when towing a pontoon on 10 November 2012. One source claims that it was a different tug named *Atoll* but that seems to be incorrect. We see *Capt I B Harvey* again on page 43.

(Peter Hobday)

Another Russian-built tug in the fleet of West Coast Towing was the **E L Preston**. She was constructed as **Imakon I** at the Gorokhovets shipyard and is powered by two 8-cylinder Pervomaysk engines each of 802bhp driving two controllable pitch propellers. These are protected against ice beneath waterline. She is another example of Project 04983 design, with the type name Anton Mazin also being given. A large number of these tugs were built for Russian navy. She passes Battery Point on 11 April 1997. Renamed **Butegarth** in 2002, she became **Vega 1** in 2003 and, following return to Russian ownership, **Poseydon** in 2004. She is owned by Anship (Anrusstrans) based at Kavkaz.

(Bernard McCall)

The **Capt I B Harvey** was built at Gorokhovets Shipyard on the River Volga as **Vik III**. She and a sister tug were bought by Norwegian owners but both were laid up at Stavanger and were eventually sold for operation by West Coast Towing (UK) Ltd and towed to Newport, arriving on 24 February 1994. She was soon renamed **Capt I B Harvey**. She is also powered by two 8-cylinder Pervomaysk engines, each of 802bhp, and geared to two controllable pitch propellers in Kort-type nozzles. She has a 25 tonne bollard pull. West Coast Towing (UK) Ltd also entered the market for ocean towage and acquired some vessels for this purpose. The company also felt that there was a niche for a smaller vessel in the coastal towing market and so although acquired as a harbour tug, the **Capt I B Harvey** was refitted as a coastal towing vessel in 2002. She was fitted for her new role with a double drum towing winch, hydraulic deck crane, extra navigational aids and fresh water capacity and she was soon in demand by dredging and civil engineering companies. With a barge in tow, she passes Battery Point on 17 January 2004. In summer 2002 she was chartered to tow floating cages in support of the tuna fishing fleet in the Mediterranean. In 2005 she was sold to operators based in Abu Dhabi and was renamed **Al Jaber II**.

(Bernard McCall)

The **Valiant Nader** was built as a tug/supply ship by Brodogradiliste "Tito" Beograd at Macvanska Mitrovica in the former Yugoslavia. Built as **Sea Diamond**. she became **Chambon Bora** in 1984 and was then sold to the Alexandra Towing Company and converted to a tug. She was the third of three sister vessels and, to be renamed **Indefatigable**, was handed over in Port de Bouc in southern France. The delivery crew came from Swansea and taking over the ship had its fair share of problems. Not only was she infested with cockroaches after being in the Persian Gulf for the previous five years, but she was targeted by thieves as the new crew slept on board. Power comes from two Alpha diesels, each of 2480bhp and geared to two controllable pitch propellers in steerable Kort nozzles, giving her a bollard pull of 70 tonnes. On arrival in the UK, the vessel was drydocked at Sheerness for a minor refit. Based at Swansea, she transferred to the Thames in February 1986 and was renamed **Avenger**. Sold to West Coast Towing and renamed **Valiant Nader** in 1994, she undertook many ocean tows for this company until sold in 2003 to Wllbros Marine, of Houston, Texas, by whom she was renamed **WB-Force 1**. We see her towing the barge **Karlissa B** to Lowestoft, the barge having been used in the production of concrete that was poured into the caissons of the new Severn road bridge, the construction of which is visible in the distance.

(Danny Lynch)

The **Alice K** was another of the tugs acquired from Russia by West Coast Towing. She was completed at the Gorokhovets shipyard in May 1994 and may possibly have been named *Project 269* when launched. Like the *E L Preston*, she has two 8-cylinder Pervomaysk engines but of slightly less power being 799bhp, the engines being geared to two controllable pitch propellers. She has a bollard pull of 25 tonnes. She was purchased along with another Russian tug by her owners and a condition of sale was that the pair had to be delivered outside Russian waters. As a result both were collected in Finnish waters outside Vyborg by another tug from the fleet of West Coast Towing and the three vessels arrived in the UK on 5 August 1995. She returned to Russian ownership in 2005 when bought by an operator in the port of Kandalaksha and renamed *Gandvik*. She was heading for drydock at Sharpness when she passed Battery Point on 16 March 2003. By this time, West Coast Towing had been taken over by Wijsmuller and this company itself was quickly taken over by Svitzer.

(Dominic McCall)

The **Duke of Normandy II** has a fascinating history. She was built in 1934 as **Ems**, and was used by the German customs service to transport personnel. She was requisitioned by the Kriegsmarine as a harbour protection vessel during World War II. She was stationed in Jersey as part of the German occupation of the Channel Islands and with other units she took part in two German raids on the French port of Granville in February and March 1945. In May 1945, she carried the name **F.K.O.1** when she was taken over as war reparations remaining in the Channel Islands until sale to the States of Jersey in 1949 being renamed **Duke of Normandy**. In 1958 her original Deutz engine of 375bhp was replaced by a Mirrlees of 290bhp. She was sold and renamed **Duke of Normandy II** in 1972 and by 1974 she was classed as a DTI Class 9 workboat in the ownership of a company in Arrochar. In 1992 she was bought by Nick Walker, owner of **VIC 32**, but appeared on the sale lists in 2013. We see her at the International Festival of the Sea in the City Docks in May 1996.

(Bernard McCall)

Hidden by the **Duke of Normandy** in the previous image is the **Brocklebank**. The Alexandra Towing Co Ltd was founded in Liverpool in 1887. In 1919 it established a base in Southampton and another in Swansea six years later. The company expanded rapidly in the mid-1960s, thanks to several takeovers and the acquisition of newbuildings. In 1964, it placed orders for six similar tugs, three to be built at Hessle for the Solent fleet and three at the Yarwood shipyard in Northwich for the Mersey fleet. Launched on 28 August 1964, the **Brocklebank** was the second of the Yarwood tugs. Power comes from a Crossley engine of 1200bhp geared to a single propeller and provides a bollard pull of 18 tonnes. Although working mainly on the River Mersey, she worked at other ports in the north-west of England such as Heysham and Barrow-in-Furness. She also towed barges filled with stone from Dinmore Quarry on Anglesey to Liverpool for use in the construction of Seaforth dock. Taken out of service in 1988 she was acquired by Merseyside Maritime Museum and is claimed to be the only seagoing vessel owned by a maritime museum in the UK. She has become a regular visitor to the Bristol Harbour Festival and we see her on 21 July 2014 as she is about to pass beneath the Clifton Suspension Bridge on her return to Liverpool.

(Bernard McCall)

We now look at a selection of tugs that have been used to assist the local fleet in ship-handling. The *Thrax* was photographed on 15 May 2014 after assisting the bulk carrier *Saronic Trader* into Royal Portbury Dock. She was built by Simek at Flekkefjord in Norway and is driven by two 6-cylinder Wärtsilä Wichmann engines, each of 2447bhp and geared to two directional propellers. This combination gives her a bollard pull of 62 tonnes. In 2009 the *Thrax* was awarded the contract to serve the ConocoPhillips Ireland oil terminal at Bantry Bay in the south of the Republic of Ireland. This contract was initially for one year, commencing on 1 November 2009. The contract has been renewed annually since that time. Her owning company, Østensjø Rederi, was established in 1973 and initially operated only supply vessels but in 1984 it won the contract to service tankers visiting the huge new gas terminal at Kårsto near Haugesund in Norway. Since then, the company has been at the forefront of towage services for the oil industry.

(Chris Jones)

The remaining tugs come from the Cory and Svitzer fleets. In 1986 Cory won a contract to provide towage services at Puerto Armuelles in Panama. At first chartered vessels were used, but in 1986 a contract was placed with Cochrane Shipbuilders for two purpose-built tugs to be named *Maria Isabelle* and *Maria Luisa*. Unfortunately, these names already existed on the Panamanian ship register and consequently *Maria Isabelle* became *Maria Isabelle I* and *Maria Luisa* became *Maria Luisa II*. After the contract was ended she was laid up at Willemstad and later chartered by Smit International for work in Panama. Currently owned in Argentina, she is based at Bahia Blanca. She passes Battery Point in May 2000, a very rare visitor indeed.

(Bernard McCall)

The **Hurricane H** is a tug with an interesting history. She was the second of a pair of tugs built for Alexandra Towing Co Ltd at the Richard Dunston shipyard in Hessle to handle the large ore carriers using what was the new tidal harbour at Port Talbot. After almost 27 years of excellent service she was sold to West Coast Towing which, surprisingly, won the contract to supply towage services at the Port Talbot tidal harbour from February 1997. Renamed **Hurricane H**, she continued to do the work for which she had been built and did so from 2001 when Wijsmuller took over West Coast Towing. In 2008 she was bought by a Greek company and renamed **Voukefalas**. In late 2015 she was reported to be at Berbera in the Gulf of Aden. We see her passing Battery Point in rapidly-fading light on 8 February 2003.

(Bernard McCall)

Ordered by Cory Towage, the **Ayton Cross** was the first of two sister tugs built by Astilleros Zamakona at Santurtzi near Bilbao. She was launched 3 April 2000 and delivered on 27 October. Wijsmuller took over Cory Towage during the construction of the tugs. Her name (and that of sister tug **Ormesby Cross**) indicated that both were intended for work on the River Tees and indeed the **Ayton Cross** duly arrived on the Tees in December 2000. She transferred to the Mersey in 2005 and then to the Clyde in late 2007. She was also a popular tug for coastal towage and in this role has been noted at Portsmouth where she collected a barge containing parts for the new aircraft carrier being built at Rosyth. Her bollard pull is 55 tonnes. Power comes from two Niigata 6-cylinder engines with a total output of 4400bhp and driving two Z-peller propulsion units. Hot air balloons are just coming into view in the distance.

(Kevin Jones)

The **Dalegarth** was built for its own account by Hanasaki Zosensho at Yokosuka in Japan. Launched on 5 March 1985, she was to have been named **Yokosuka Maru No. 1** but at a late stage in her construction she was bought by J P Knight, of Rochester, and was completed for that company as **Kestrel** on 15 March 1985 although delivery was delayed until December. Soon after arrival in the UK she was chartered by Cory Towage to service a contract at Puerto Armuelles in Panama. After being replaced by the purpose-built **Maria Luisa II** (see page 49), she was transferred to the Pajaritos terminal in Mexico. In 1990 she was purchased by Cory Towage and renamed **Strongbow**. She returned to the UK from Mexico in August 1991 and was placed initially in the Mersey fleet but she was transferred to Milford Haven and renamed **Dalegarth** in 1992. Like many tugs built in Japan, she is powered by two 6-cylinder Niigata engines with a total output of 3200bhp and geared to two multidirectional Z-peller units. This gives her a bollard pull of 45 tonnes. Sold out of the fleet to owners in Romania in autumn 2015, she was transferred to the Romanian flag and renamed **LRS Europa**. She now works in the Black Sea usually in the Constanta area.

(Kevin Jones)

The **Yewgarth**, photographed late in the evening of 14 August 2007, followed the **Oakgarth** from McTay Marine at Bromborough. She was launched on 9 January 1985 and delivered to Cory Ship Towage on 29 March. Her two 6-cylinder Ruston engines with a total of 4000bhp were each connected to a Z-peller unit and this gave her a bollard pull of 50 tonnes. On entry into service, she was sent to work on a new Cory contract at Puerto Bolivar in Colombia and thence to the Pajaritos oil terminal in Mexico. In January 1992 she left the US Gulf to take up a charter in Dubai. In the UK, she worked mainly on the River Mersey but in 1996, she moved to Milford Haven to provide cover for local tugs involved in the salvage of the tanker **Sea Empress**. Latterly she was based in South Wales as part of the Svitzer fleet. Although laid up with crankcase damage, in October 2012 she was sold to Black Sea Services in Constanta and was renamed **BSV Irlandia**. She and another former Svitzer tug were towed from Swansea Bay by the **Pantodynamos** on 11 November 2012.

(Kevin Jones)

The **Millgarth** was one of a pair of tugs ordered by Cory in the mid-1990s for the Milford Haven fleet. She was the second of the pair to be delivered, following the **Anglegarth**. Her hull was subcontracted to Stocznia Polnocna (Northern Shipyard) at Gdansk in Poland. The hull, of the standard Damen ASD3211 design, was launched on 28 September 1996 and towed to the Damen yard in Gorinchem for completion. Handed over on 19 February 1997, the **Millgarth** arrived in Milford Haven four days later. Power comes from two 6-cylinder Stork-Wärtsilä engines, each of 2583bhp and geared to two z-peller units within fixed Kort nozzles. This arrangement gives her a bollard pull of 66 tonnes. She left Milford Haven on 4 October 2009 and headed for the Medway for a short stay before starting work on the Thames. Apart from a brief sojourn on the Tees between 18 February and 23 March 2012, she stayed on the Thames until leaving for the Mersey on 10 April 2014. She diverted to the Bristol Channel on the evening of 12 April to assist with the docking of the bulk carrier **Trans Nanjing** in the early hours of the next day. This was the only occasion that she worked in the Bristol Channel.

(Bernard McCall)

The **Flying Spindrift** was launched at the Richard Dunston shipyard in Hessle on 28 October 1985 and delivered to the Clyde Shipping Company on 31 January 1986. She is driven by two Ruston engines, each of 1550bhp geared to two stern-mounted Aquamaster units incorporating a Kort nozzle. This gives her a bollard pull of 38 tonnes. She incorporated several novel features which have since become commonplace in tugs. The wheelhouse, for example, was intended for operation by one person and incorporated several features to enable this. These included a foot-operated radio switch to enable full communication even when the master may be otherwise fully occupied. In 1994 she was transferred to Lawson-Batey Tugs, Newcastle, and in May of the following year was taken over by Cory Towage. She passed through the ownership of Wijsmuller and Svitzer, the latter transferring her to its Felixarc Marine subsidiary in 2009. In June 2012 she was sold to Farsund Fortøyningsselskap, Farsund, Norway, and renamed **FFS Atlas** under the St Vincent & Grenadines flag. She left Lowestoft for Farsund on 30 June 2012.

(Kevin Jones)

The **Svitzer Melton** began life as part of an £18 million newbuilding programme for Howard Smith. Her hull was built by Stocznia Polnocna SA (Northern Shipyard) at Gdansk with completion at the Damen shipyard in Gorinchem. Delivered in May 1996 to work as **Melton** in the Felixstowe fleet. She is an example of the ASD 321 design. She is powered by two 6-cylinder Ruston engines each of 2447bhp and each connected to a Z-peller unit. This gives her a bollard pull of 55 tonnes. Results on trials exceeded expectations. Although ownership was transferred to Adsteam after that company took over Howard Smith, she was never given an Adsteam name but rather became **Svitzer Melton** in late 2007. She was photographed as she attended the **Saronic Trader** on 19 June 2014.

(Bernard McCall)

The **Svitzer Lyndhurst** was part of that same building programme as Svitzer Melton. She was launched at the Bromborough shipyard of McTay Marine on 8 February 1996 and delivered as **Lyndhurst** to Howard Smith Towage on 12 April. Although transferred to Adsteam Towage in 2001, it was not until 2006 that she was renamed **Adsteam Lyndhurst** and then **Svitzer Lyndhurst** in 2009 after Adsteam had been taken over by Svitzer two years previously. As her name suggests, she was intended for service in the Southampton area. Ousted from the Solent in late 2009, she was transferred to the Tyne fleet and then in mid-March 2013 she arrived in the Firth of Forth. Power comes from two 6-cylinder Ruston engines each of 2008bhp and geared to two Voith-Schneider propellers. Her bollard pull is 43 tonnes. On 3 April 2010, she was the bow tug for the bulk carrier **Bottiglieri Challenger** which was delivering coal from Richards Bay to Royal Portbury Dock at the end of her maiden commercial voyage. The **Svitzer Lyndhurst** assisted a departing ship on the same tide, her only day on the Bristol Channel.

(Bernard McCall)

The year 2009 saw the opening of two new terminals on Milford Haven for the import of liquefied natural gas delivered by large gas tankers. The towage contract to handle these tankers was won by Svitzer and nine new powerful tugs were built. Three of these were designed by Svitzer themselves and built at the Qingdao Qianin shipyard in China. All three, known as the "Wick" class, were intended to work at the South Hook LNG terminal and so had red-topped funnels in order to distinguish them from the other tugs. The **Svitzer Musselwick** was launched on 12 March 2008 and delivered on 9 August. We see **Svitzer Musselwick** assisting a bulk carrier soon after the morning mist had cleared on 5 March 2013.

(Bernard McCall)

The **Svitzer Gelliswick** is another of the "Wick" class tugs built by Qingdao Qianjin shipyard. They are slightly less powerful than the other six new tugs built at Vigo. Power comes from two 8-cylinder Niigata engines with a total output of 5998bhp and geared to two z-peller units; this combination gives a bollard pull of 89 tonnes. All three were delivered under their own power and the long delivery voyage is sometimes blamed for the need to send them to Vigo for "repair and modification". The **Svitzer Gelliswick** was launched on 19 February 2008 and delivered during August. She was pushing alongside a bulk carrier when photographed from Battery Point on 11 October 2012.

(Bernard McCall)

Six of the nine new tugs for Milford Haven were built by Construcciones Navales P Freire at Vigo in Spain, one being the **Svitzer Lindsway**. Launched on 8 May 2008, she was delivered on 30 October. She is driven by two General Electric engines generating a total of 7880bhp and powering two Schottel fully steerable propulsion units. On trials she achieved a bollard pull of over 100 tonnes, some 10% greater than the contracted 92 tonnes. It will be noticed that her funnel has a red top. The reason for this is that she was dedicated to handling ships for Qatargas at the South Hook lng terminal on Milford Haven. She was photographed on 3 November 2014.

(Kevin Jones)

The **Svitzer Waterston**, another of the Milford Haven tugs, is a sister of the **Svitzer Lindsway**. Designed by Robert Allan Ltd, this pair and the three fitted with General Electric engines, have been designated the RA star 3400 class. Launched on 15 February 2008 and delivered on 1 August 2008, she was the first of the class to arrive in Milford Haven. She had an unfortunate entry into service. On 2 August, the day after her arrival, she underwent propulsion trials in the Haven with her new master on board accompanied by two other masters taking the opportunity to familiarise themselves with the new vessel. During the trials, various alarms sounded and lack of familiarisation caused delays in cancelling these. The tug grounded briefly after completion of the trials but extensive damage was caused to the port propulsion unit. She has had short periods of work beyond Milford Haven, notably on the Clyde and on the Mersey during 2010/2011.

(Kevin Jones)

The **Svitzer Caldey**, photographed on 20 October 2014, is another of the six tugs designed for service at Milford Haven and built by Construcciones Navales P Freire at Vigo. She differs from the **Svitzer Lindsway** in having a Niigata propulsion system. Her two 8-cylinder Niigata engines with a total output of 5998bhp are geared to two Z-peller propulsion units with fixed pitch propellers. She and sister tug **Svitzer Ramsey** have a bollard pull of 82 tonnes.

(Kevin Jones)

The **Svitzer Keelby** came to the UK because of the Adsteam connection. She was built in Newcastle, New South Wales, by Carrington Slipways Pty Ltd. She was launched on 12 December 1985, and delivered as **W J Trotter** on 30 May 1986 to the Queensland Tug and Salvage Company with Howard Smith as managers. In 2001, Adsteam took over ownership and she was renamed **Redcliffe**. As Redcliffe Bay is part of Portishead, she is an appropriate tug to be seen in the area. She was transferred to the UK in 2004 and worked on the River Thames as **Redcliffe** but was renamed **Adsteam Keelby** in 2005, becoming **Svitzer Keelby** in late April 2007. She is driven by two 8-cylinder Yanmar engines, each of 2401bhp and driving two Z-peller units. This combination gives her a bollard pull of 67 tonnes. She was photographed on 19 September 2012. In early 2015 she was sold to operators in the British Virgin Islands and renamed **Keelby** under the Comoros flag. At the time of writing she is working in the Ukrainian port of Yuzhny.

(Bernard McCall)

It is appropriate that we close with another view of the **Bristolian**. She is usually to be found moored amongst other smaller vessels at Underfall Yard in the City Docks. The best opportunity to see her working is when the **Balmoral** is moving. Perhaps surprisingly, she does not usually assist the **Balmoral** in the River Avon but she is always on hand when the latter vessel is moving in or out of the City Docks. She is seen near the lock entrance on such an occasion on 11 July 2015.

(Bernard McCall)